Table of Contents

2023 Digital Gold Rush: Unleashing the Best Online Business Ideas and Niches From

the Comfort of Your Home

Chapter 1: The Digital Landscape: Opportunities Galore

Introduction to the Digital Economy

The digital economy is an expansive, ever-evolving frontier of opportunities that has fundamentally transformed how we live, work, and conduct business. At its core, the digital economy encompasses all economic activities that rely on digital technologies, spanning various sectors including e-commerce, online services, digital content, and more. This transformation has been fueled by the advent of the internet and the proliferation of digital devices, enabling businesses to operate, market, and sell their products and services to a global audience with unprecedented ease. One of the most compelling aspects of the digital economy is its low barrier to entry. Unlike traditional brick-and-mortar businesses, starting an online business often requires significantly less capital investment. Entrepreneurs can launch websites, leverage social media, and utilize online marketplaces to reach customers worldwide without the need for physical storefronts or extensive inventory. This democratization of business startup opportunities has paved the way for individuals from all walks of life to explore their entrepreneurial ambitions.

Furthermore, the global reach of the digital economy means that businesses are no longer confined to their geographical locations. An online store can sell products to customers thousands of miles away, a digital content creator can amass a global audience, and a service provider can offer solutions to clients across continents. This unparalleled access to a worldwide market has enabled businesses to scale at a pace and scope that were unimaginable in the pre-digital era.

Why Now?

We are currently living in what can only be described as a golden age for digital entrepreneurship. Several factors converge to make this an ideal time to venture into the online business world:

- **Technological Advancements**: Rapid advancements in technology have made sophisticated tools and platforms accessible to the average person. From e-commerce platforms and digital marketing tools to cloud computing and mobile technology, it's easier than ever to create, manage, and grow an online business.

- **Societal Shifts**: Changes in consumer behavior, accelerated by the COVID-19 pandemic, have led to an increased reliance on online services for shopping, entertainment, education, and work. This shift has opened up new avenues for businesses to meet the growing demand for digital offerings.
- **Increased Connectivity**: The expansion of internet access and the rise of mobile internet usage have brought billions of people online, significantly expanding the potential customer base for online businesses.

These factors, combined with a growing ecosystem of support resources for digital entrepreneurs, from online courses to networking communities, create a fertile ground for launching and growing online businesses.

Success Potential

The potential for success in the digital economy is not just theoretical; it's evidenced by countless success stories and backed by compelling statistics. Consider the following:

- **E-commerce Growth**: According to Statista, global e-commerce sales are expected to reach new highs, with projections suggesting a continued upward trend. This growth indicates a robust and expanding market for online retailers.

- **Freelancing and Remote Work**: Platforms like Upwork and Fiverr have reported significant increases in usage, as more people turn to freelancing and remote work opportunities. This trend reflects the expanding market for digital services and the freelance economy.

- **Digital Content Consumption**: The surge in online content consumption, from streaming services to online courses, highlights the growing demand for digital content across various formats and niches.

Success stories abound, from solo entrepreneurs who have built lucrative online stores to content creators who have turned their passions into profitable careers, and service providers who have scaled their operations to serve clients globally. These stories underscore the potential for financial prosperity and personal fulfillment in the digital realm.

In conclusion, the digital landscape offers a world of opportunities for those willing to explore it. With the right approach, knowledge, and perseverance, the digital economy presents a promising avenue for entrepreneurial success and financial independence. As we delve deeper into the nuances of starting and growing an online business in the following chapters, remember that the potential for success in this digital gold rush is limited only by your imagination, effort, and willingness to adapt and learn.

Chapter 2: The Blueprint for Online Success

Embarking on an online business venture requires more than just a great idea or a unique product—it demands a specific mindset and skill set, a solid foundation from which to grow, and strategies to overcome inevitable challenges. This chapter delves into the core elements that constitute the blueprint for online success, guiding you through the initial steps of establishing your digital enterprise, nurturing its growth, and ensuring its sustainability in the face of obstacles.

Mindset and Skills

Adaptability: The digital landscape is in constant flux, with new technologies emerging, consumer preferences evolving, and competitive landscapes shifting. Success in this environment necessitates adaptability—the ability to pivot quickly in response to market changes or challenges. Entrepreneurs must stay informed about industry trends, be open to revising their strategies, and be willing to experiment with new ideas.

Continuous Learning: The fast-paced nature of the digital world means that there's always something new to learn. Whether it's the latest in digital marketing strategies, new tools for optimizing your online store, or updates on data privacy laws, staying ahead requires an ongoing commitment to education. Embrace online courses, webinars, podcasts, and other resources to continually enhance your knowledge and skills.

Resilience: The journey of an online entrepreneur is filled with ups and downs. Projects might fail, campaigns might not yield expected results, and growth might stall. Resilience—the ability to bounce back from setbacks—is crucial. Cultivate a positive mindset, learn from failures, and view challenges as opportunities to grow and improve.

Building a Foundation

Choosing the Right Business Model: The foundation of a successful online business is a viable, sustainable business model. Consider the various models available—e-commerce, subscription services, SaaS (Software as a Service), content creation, affiliate marketing, and more. Evaluate each model's fit with your skills, interests, and the market demand. Ensure that your chosen model aligns with your long-term goals and has the potential for scalability.

Understanding Your Target Audience: Knowing who your customers are, what they need, and how they behave online is pivotal. Conduct market research to gain insights into your audience's demographics, preferences, pain points, and purchasing behavior. This understanding will inform your product development, marketing strategies, and customer service approaches, making them more effective.

Creating Value: In the crowded digital marketplace, standing out requires offering unique value to your customers. This could be through innovative products, exceptional service, valuable content, or a unique customer experience. Always ask yourself how your business can solve a problem, fulfill a need, or enhance your customers' lives in a way that no one else is doing.

Overcoming Obstacles

Dealing with Competition: The digital world's low barriers to entry mean that competition is fierce. Differentiate your business through branding, niche targeting, and by offering unparalleled value. Use competitive analysis to understand your rivals' strengths and weaknesses, and carve out your unique selling proposition (USP) to stand out.

Navigating Technology Issues: Technology is the backbone of any online business, but it can also be a source of frustration and challenges. To mitigate technology risks, invest in reliable platforms and tools, ensure your website is secure and user-friendly, and have a contingency plan for outages or data loss. Stay informed about technological advancements and be ready to upgrade your systems as needed.

Avoiding Burnout: Entrepreneurial burnout is a real risk, especially when you're juggling multiple roles. To prevent burnout, prioritize work-life balance, set realistic goals, delegate tasks when possible, and take regular breaks. Remember, sustaining your health and well-being is just as important as growing your business.

In conclusion, the blueprint for online success is multifaceted, requiring a combination of the right mindset, a solid business foundation, and strategies to navigate inevitable challenges. By cultivating adaptability, embracing continuous learning, building resilience, carefully choosing your business model, understanding your audience, creating value, and effectively dealing with competition, technology issues, and the risk of burnout, you'll be well on your way to establishing a thriving online business. Remember, the journey of entrepreneurship is a marathon, not a sprint—patience, persistence, and perseverance are key.

Chapter 3: Trends and Insights: Uncovering the Hottest Niches

In the ever-evolving digital economy, identifying and capitalizing on emerging trends can set the foundation for a successful online business. This chapter explores promising niches with significant growth potential, guides you through conducting effective market analysis, and unveils strategies for discovering untapped opportunities in the digital marketplace.

Promising Niches

Sustainable Products: The growing awareness and concern for the environment have led to an increased demand for sustainable and eco-friendly products. This niche spans various categories, from fashion and beauty to home goods and technology. Businesses that focus on sustainability not only cater to a growing market segment but also contribute positively to the planet.

Home Fitness: The shift towards home-based fitness routines, accelerated by the COVID-19 pandemic, has opened up vast opportunities in the online fitness sector. This includes the sale of home fitness equipment, virtual fitness classes, and personal training services. With health and wellness becoming a top priority for many, this niche offers a wide array of opportunities for online businesses.

Remote Work Solutions: As remote work becomes the new norm for many companies worldwide, there's a rising demand for products and services that facilitate this transition. This includes software for project management and communication, ergonomic home office furniture, and online courses that teach remote work skills. Catering to the needs of remote workers and businesses can carve out a lucrative niche in the current market.

Market Analysis

Understanding market trends, consumer behavior, and competition is crucial for identifying and exploiting business opportunities. Here's how to conduct a thorough market analysis:

Trend Monitoring: Keep abreast of industry trends by following relevant news sources, industry blogs, and reports. Tools like Google Trends can also provide valuable insights into what's gaining popularity over time.

Consumer Behavior: Dive into consumer forums, social media, and review sites to understand your target audience's needs, preferences, and pain points. Surveys and polls can also provide direct feedback from potential customers.

Competitive Analysis: Analyze your competition by examining their product offerings, marketing strategies, customer reviews, and social media activity. Identify gaps in their offerings or areas where your business could offer superior value.

Finding Untapped Opportunities

Innovation and creativity are key to uncovering niches that are ripe for development. Here are strategies to find those hidden gems:

Solve a Problem: Look for common frustrations or problems faced by people in your target market. If there's a widespread issue that lacks an effective solution, you may have found your niche.

Niche Down: Consider nichifying further within a broader market. For example, instead of targeting the entire fitness market, focus on a specific demographic, like fitness for new mothers or busy professionals.

Leverage Emerging Technologies: Stay informed about the latest technological advancements and think about how they can be applied to create new products or services. For example, how can augmented reality (AR) enhance the online shopping experience for your niche?

Cross-Industry Inspiration: Sometimes, the best ideas come from looking outside your industry. Can a successful concept in one industry be adapted to serve an unmet need in another?

In conclusion, finding the right niche requires a combination of market research, trend analysis, creative thinking, and a deep understanding of consumer needs. By identifying areas of significant growth potential, such as sustainable products, home fitness, and remote work solutions, and employing strategies to analyze the market and uncover untapped opportunities, you can position your online business for success in the competitive digital landscape. Remember, the key is to stay agile, informed, and always on the lookout for the next big thing.

Chapter 4: E-commerce Empires: Mastering the Online Retail Space

The e-commerce sector has witnessed explosive growth, offering entrepreneurs a lucrative avenue to build their empires from the comfort of their homes. This chapter explores the intricacies of e-commerce, from selecting the right business model to carving out a niche and implementing strategies that drive success.

Business Models

Dropshipping: This model allows you to sell products without holding any inventory. When a customer places an order, the product is shipped directly from the supplier to the customer.

Pros: Low startup costs and minimal risk, as you don't need to purchase inventory upfront. It also offers the flexibility to test products and markets with little financial commitment.

Cons: Lower profit margins, limited control over shipping and product quality, and intense competition.

Print-on-Demand (POD): Similar to dropshipping, POD allows you to sell customized products (e.g., t-shirts, mugs) without inventory. The product is printed and shipped to the customer once an order is made.

Pros: Offers customization and personalization options for your products, leading to unique offerings. Like dropshipping, it has low startup costs and inventory risks.

Cons: Limited to products that can be printed on, and per-unit costs can be higher, potentially reducing margins.

Stocking Inventory: This traditional e-commerce model involves purchasing and holding stock, which you then sell to customers.

Pros: Higher profit margins, greater control over product selection, quality, and shipping times.

Cons: Higher initial investment and risk, as you need to purchase and manage inventory. There's also the challenge of inventory forecasting and storage.

Niche-Specific Ventures

Selecting a niche is crucial for building a strong brand and attracting a loyal customer base in the vast e-commerce marketplace. A well-defined niche allows you to tailor your product offerings, marketing efforts, and customer experience to a specific audience, enhancing your competitive advantage. It also simplifies decision-making regarding inventory, branding, and marketing strategies. When choosing a niche, consider factors like market demand, competition level, and your personal interests or expertise.

Strategies for Success

Product Sourcing: Your e-commerce success significantly depends on finding reliable suppliers that offer quality products at competitive prices. Explore options like domestic wholesalers, overseas manufacturers, or POD services. Attend trade shows, use online marketplaces, and conduct thorough research to vet potential suppliers.

Search Engine Optimization (SEO): SEO is critical for driving organic traffic to your e-commerce store. Optimize your website and product pages with relevant keywords, high-quality images, and engaging product descriptions. Ensure your site has a mobile-friendly design and fast loading times to improve user experience and search engine rankings.

Social Media Marketing: Social media platforms are powerful tools for building brand awareness, engaging with customers, and driving sales. Choose platforms where your target audience is most active, and create content that entertains, informs, and educates. Leverage social media ads for targeted campaigns to boost traffic and conversions.

Customer Service: Exceptional customer service can set your e-commerce business apart from the competition. Offer multiple channels for customer support (e.g., live chat, email, phone), and strive to provide quick and helpful responses. Implementing a hassle-free return policy and actively seeking customer feedback can also enhance satisfaction and loyalty.

In conclusion, mastering the online retail space requires careful consideration of your business model, a strategic approach to niche selection, and the implementation of effective strategies for product sourcing, SEO, social media marketing, and customer service. By focusing on these key areas, you can build a successful e-commerce empire that stands out in the competitive digital marketplace.

Chapter 5: Content Creation: Transforming Passion into Profit

In the digital age, content creation has emerged as a powerful avenue for transforming personal passions, hobbies, and expertise into profitable online businesses. This chapter delves into the essentials of monetizing your knowledge through various content formats, exploring creative revenue streams and offering insights into the burgeoning world of podcasting.

Monetizing Expertise

Turning Knowledge into Content: The first step in monetizing your expertise is to identify your niche—be it in fitness, cooking, technology, or any other field—and decide on the content format that best suits your skills and audience preferences. Blogs, YouTube channels, and podcasts are popular platforms that cater to different types of content and audiences.

- **Blogs**: Ideal for writers who can convey expertise through articles, guides, and tutorials. Blogs can be monetized through advertising, affiliate marketing, and sponsored content.

- **YouTube**: Perfect for those comfortable in front of a camera and skilled in video production. Revenue can be generated through ad earnings, sponsorships, and by directing viewers to paid products or services.
- **Podcasts**: Suitable for individuals who excel in storytelling and verbal communication. Podcasts can be monetized through sponsorships, memberships, and merchandise.

Building an Audience: Consistently creating high-quality, valuable content is crucial for building and retaining an audience. Engage with your audience through comments, social media, and email newsletters. Use SEO techniques for blogs, optimize video titles and descriptions on YouTube, and promote your podcasts across various platforms to increase visibility.

Creativity and Monetization

Advertising and Sponsorships: These are common monetization methods across all content platforms. Secure sponsorships by reaching out to brands within your niche that align with your audience's interests. Display ads on your blog or website can generate revenue based on traffic.

Merchandise: Selling branded merchandise is an excellent way to monetize a loyal fan base. Items such as t-shirts, mugs, and stickers can be created with minimal upfront costs using print-on-demand services.

Membership Models: Platforms like Patreon allow content creators to offer exclusive content, perks, and interactions in exchange for a monthly membership fee. This model builds a community around your content and provides a steady income stream.

The World of Podcasting

Growing Popularity: Podcasting has seen a meteoric rise in popularity, offering a unique way to connect with audiences on a personal level. Topics can range from niche hobbies to broad subjects like business or health, catering to a wide array of interests.

Equipment and Setup: Starting a podcast requires minimal equipment, with a good quality microphone, headphones, and audio editing software being the essentials. As your podcast grows, you can invest in more advanced equipment and professional editing services.

Monetization Strategies: Besides sponsorships and advertisements, podcasts can be monetized by promoting affiliate products, offering paid memberships for exclusive content, and selling merchandise. Collaborations with other podcasters and cross-promotion can also help grow your audience and open up new monetization opportunities.

In conclusion, content creation offers a dynamic and fulfilling path to online entrepreneurship. By leveraging your expertise, choosing the right platforms, and employing creative monetization strategies, you can transform your passion into a profitable venture. Podcasting, in particular, represents a growing segment with vast potential for those ready to share their voice with the world. With dedication, consistency, and engagement, content creators can build a loyal audience and turn their digital presence into a thriving online business.

Chapter 6: Digital Services: Providing Value at Your Fingertips

In the vast expanse of the digital economy, providing digital services stands out as a highly adaptable and lucrative path. This chapter explores the realm of freelancing and digital service provision, from leveraging platforms and identifying in-demand skills to scaling your business into a full-fledged digital agency or consultancy.

Freelancing Platforms

Top Platforms for Freelancers: Websites like Upwork, Freelancer, Fiverr, and LinkedIn ProFinder have become the go-to destinations for freelancers seeking opportunities. Each platform caters to a wide range of services, including writing, graphic design, programming, and digital marketing.

How to Stand Out: Given the competitive nature of these platforms, differentiating yourself is crucial. Create a compelling profile that highlights your expertise, experience, and portfolio. Client testimonials can significantly boost your credibility. Consistently delivering high-quality work on time can help you build a strong reputation, leading to more and better opportunities.

In-Demand Services

The digital landscape is continually evolving, with certain skills rising in demand as businesses seek to enhance their online presence and operations.

Digital Marketing: With the digitalization of business, expertise in SEO, content marketing, PPC (pay-per-click) advertising, and social media marketing is highly sought after. Businesses need skilled professionals who can help them increase their online visibility and engagement.

Web Development: As the backbone of the internet, web development remains a critical service. Skills in building and maintaining websites, especially with knowledge of HTML, CSS, JavaScript, and back-end development languages, are in high demand.

Graphic Design: Visual content plays a pivotal role in digital marketing and branding. Graphic designers with the ability to create eye-catching logos, social media graphics, and other marketing materials are highly valued.

Scaling Your Business

From Solo Freelancing to Digital Agency: Transitioning from a solo freelancer to running a digital agency involves moving from working in the business to working on the business. This means hiring other freelancers or employees to handle client work while you focus on acquiring clients, managing projects, and scaling operations.

Offering Consulting Services: As you build expertise and establish a reputation in your field, consulting can be a lucrative next step. Consulting involves providing expert advice to businesses and requires a deep understanding of your niche, problem-solving skills, and the ability to strategize and plan effectively.

Building Your Brand: Whether scaling to an agency or moving into consulting, building a strong personal or business brand is essential. A well-defined brand helps attract the right clients and establishes you as an authority in your field. Focus on content marketing, networking, and leveraging social proof through client testimonials and case studies.

In conclusion, the digital services sector offers immense potential for growth and profitability. By understanding the dynamics of freelancing platforms, focusing on in-demand services, and strategically scaling your business, you can transition from offering freelance services to running a successful digital agency or consultancy. The key to success lies in continuously honing your skills, understanding market needs, and delivering exceptional value to your clients.

Chapter 7: Online Education: Empowering and Earning Simultaneously

The surge in online education has transformed the landscape of learning and teaching, offering unique opportunities for experts across various fields to share their knowledge and monetize their expertise. This chapter delves into the process of creating compelling online courses, highlights the latest trends in e-learning, and provides strategies for marketing your courses and establishing yourself as an authority in your niche.

Creating Courses

Step-by-Step Guide:

- **Identify Your Niche**: Focus on a subject you are passionate about and have expertise in. Conduct market research to ensure there is demand for your topic.
- **Outline Your Course**: Plan the structure of your course. Break down your topic into manageable modules or sections, each covering a specific aspect of the subject.
- **Design Your Content**: Decide on the format of your course content (video, text,

quizzes, interactive assignments). Use a mix to cater to different learning styles.

• **Create High-Quality Materials**: Invest time in producing high-quality videos and materials. Ensure your content is engaging, informative, and well-presented.

• **Choose a Platform**: Select an online course platform that fits your needs, such as Udemy, Coursera, Teachable, or your own website. Consider factors like revenue sharing, audience reach, and customization options.

• **Set Pricing and Launch**: Price your course competitively. Consider offering introductory discounts to attract initial learners. Promote your course through your network, social media, and relevant online communities.

E-Learning Trends

Microlearning: Bite-sized learning modules are becoming increasingly popular for their convenience and ability to fit into busy schedules. Design your courses with short, focused lessons that deliver value quickly.

Interactive Content: Interactive videos, quizzes, and simulations enhance engagement and retention. Incorporate these elements to make learning more effective and enjoyable.

Mobile Learning: With the increasing use of smartphones for learning, ensure your courses are mobile-friendly, allowing learners to access content anytime, anywhere.

Personalization: Tailoring the learning experience to individual needs and preferences is a growing trend. Use data analytics to offer personalized course recommendations and adaptive learning paths.

Online Authority

Content Marketing: Share valuable content related to your course topic through blogs, social media, webinars, and guest posting on reputable sites. This helps build your reputation as an expert and draws attention to your courses.

Leverage Testimonials and Reviews: Positive feedback from your students can be powerful in building trust and credibility. Feature testimonials prominently on your course page and marketing materials.

Engage with Your Audience: Participate in online forums, social media groups, and conferences related to your field. Answer questions, offer insights, and engage in discussions to establish yourself as a go-to expert.

Collaborate with Other Experts: Partner with other authorities in your field for joint webinars, interviews, or course offerings. This not only expands your reach but also enhances your credibility through association.

In conclusion, the online education sector offers immense opportunities for individuals to share their knowledge, help others learn, and generate income. By creating engaging and informative courses, staying abreast of e-learning trends, and strategically marketing yourself and your courses, you can establish a successful online education business and become a recognized authority in your niche. The journey to empowering others and earning simultaneously in the realm of online education is both rewarding and transformative.

Chapter 8: Affiliate Marketing: Driving Revenue through Strategic Partnerships

Affiliate marketing offers a compelling avenue for monetizing online content, leveraging strategic partnerships to drive revenue while providing value to your audience. This chapter breaks down the basics of affiliate marketing, guides you in selecting the best programs, and shares effective strategies for driving traffic and optimizing conversions.

Affiliate Marketing Basics

How It Works: Affiliate marketing is a performance-based marketing strategy where you earn commissions by promoting a company's products or services. As an affiliate, you're given a unique link to the product or service you're promoting. When someone clicks on your link and makes a purchase, you earn a commission from the sale.

Choosing Products to Promote: Select products that are relevant to your niche and resonate with your audience's interests and needs. Promoting products that you have personally used and can vouch for increases your credibility and the likelihood of conversions.

Promoting Products Effectively: Utilize various channels to promote affiliate products, including your website, blog, social media platforms, email newsletters, and YouTube videos. It's crucial to integrate your affiliate links naturally within high-quality content that adds value to your audience.

Finding Programs

Align with Your Audience and Content: Choose affiliate programs that offer products or services closely related to your content's focus area. This alignment ensures that the products you promote are of interest to your audience, increasing the potential for sales.

Research and Select Reputable Programs: Look for programs with a good reputation for quality products, reliable payment, and strong support for affiliates. Platforms like Amazon Associates, Commission Junction (CJ), and ShareASale host a wide range of affiliate programs across various niches.

Consider Commission Structure and Terms: Evaluate the commission rates, payment schedules, and any minimum payout thresholds. Also, review the cookie duration, which determines how long the referral link remains active after a potential customer clicks on it.

Traffic and Conversion
Driving Website Traffic: Enhance your website's SEO to improve organic search rankings and attract more visitors. Utilize social media to share valuable content with embedded affiliate links, and consider paid advertising to target specific demographics.
Optimizing for Conversions: Create compelling calls-to-action (CTAs) and place affiliate links strategically within your content where they are most likely to capture attention. Ensure your website is user-friendly, with fast loading times and a mobile-responsive design, to facilitate a smooth purchasing process.
Building Trust with Your Audience: Transparency is key in affiliate marketing. Disclose your affiliate relationships to your audience, assuring them that you promote products based on their value and relevance. Maintaining honesty and integrity fosters trust, which is essential for long-term success.
In conclusion, affiliate marketing can be a lucrative strategy for monetizing your online presence, provided you choose the right products, align with reputable programs, and implement effective traffic and conversion strategies. By focusing on building trust and providing value to your audience, you can

establish a successful affiliate marketing venture that benefits both you and your followers.

Chapter 9: Remote Consulting: Sharing Knowledge and Expertise Worldwide

In a world increasingly comfortable with remote interactions, the demand for remote consulting services has surged. This chapter guides you through establishing a remote consulting business, highlights industries ripe for consulting opportunities, and shares strategies for client acquisition and retention.

Remote Consulting Model

Defining Your Offer: Start by clearly defining the expertise and services you will offer. Identify the specific problems you can solve for your clients and the unique value you bring to the table. Specializing in a niche not only makes your marketing efforts more focused but also positions you as an expert in your field.

Setting Your Rates: Your pricing should reflect your expertise, the value you provide, and the market demand. Research what other consultants in your niche are charging. Consider starting with hourly rates, then transitioning to project-based or retainer models as you build your reputation.

Establishing Your Business: Create a professional website detailing your services, expertise, and client testimonials. Ensure you have the necessary tools and technology to deliver your services remotely, such as reliable video conferencing software and project management tools.

Industry Variations

IT Consulting: With businesses increasingly reliant on technology, there's a high demand for consultants who can advise on software development, cybersecurity, and IT strategy.

Business Management: Many organizations seek external expertise to optimize operations, develop growth strategies, and navigate financial planning. Specializing in areas like lean management, digital transformation, or startup growth can be particularly lucrative.

Health and Wellness: As individuals and companies pay more attention to health and wellness, opportunities abound for consultants specializing in nutrition, fitness, mental health, and corporate wellness programs.

Client Acquisition

Networking: Building a strong professional network is crucial. Attend industry conferences, join relevant online forums, and participate in webinars. Connecting with other professionals can lead to referrals and partnerships.

Online Marketing: Utilize digital marketing strategies to reach potential clients. Content marketing, through blogging or creating valuable resources, can attract clients by demonstrating your expertise. Social media and email marketing can also be effective channels for engaging potential clients.

Leveraging Social Proof: Client testimonials, case studies, and success stories are powerful tools for building credibility and trust. Feature these prominently on your website and in your marketing materials. Encouraging satisfied clients to refer others to your services can also be a significant source of new business.

Offering Free Initial Consultations: Providing a free initial consultation can be an effective way to attract new clients. It allows potential clients to experience the value of your expertise directly and establishes the foundation for a working relationship.

In conclusion, launching and growing a remote consulting business requires a strategic approach to defining your services, setting your rates, and effectively marketing your expertise. By focusing on industries where consulting is thriving and employing targeted strategies for client acquisition and retention, you can build a successful consulting practice that leverages your knowledge and skills to serve clients across the globe. The flexibility and reach of remote consulting not only empower you to share your expertise more widely but also offer the potential for a rewarding and profitable career path.

Chapter 10: The Power of Automation: Streamlining and Scaling Your Business

In today's digital age, automation stands as a cornerstone for business growth, offering unparalleled opportunities to streamline operations, enhance efficiency, and scale businesses sustainably. This chapter explores essential automation tools, the pivotal role of automation in achieving scalability, and the transformative impact of artificial intelligence (AI) on customer experience and operational efficiency.

Automation Tools

Email Marketing: Tools like Mailchimp and Constant Contact automate email campaigns, allowing businesses to schedule newsletters, promotional offers, and personalized communications with their audience, ensuring timely and relevant engagement.

Social Media Management: Platforms such as Hootsuite and Buffer enable businesses to automate their social media posts across various channels. These tools help in planning and scheduling content, analyzing engagement metrics, and managing interactions, thereby maintaining a consistent social media presence.

Customer Service: Solutions like Zendesk and Freshdesk incorporate automation to manage customer inquiries and support tickets. Automated responses to common questions and issues expedite resolution times and free up human agents for more complex queries.

E-commerce Operations: Shopify and WooCommerce offer automation features for e-commerce businesses, streamlining processes such as inventory management, order fulfillment, and payment processing, reducing manual effort and minimizing errors.

Achieving Scalability

Automation is instrumental in scaling business operations, as it enables companies to handle increased workloads without a corresponding increase in staffing costs. By automating routine tasks, businesses can allocate human resources to strategic, high-value activities that drive growth and innovation. Automation also ensures consistency and reliability in operations, critical factors for maintaining quality and customer satisfaction as a business grows.

The key to effective scalability through automation lies in identifying operational bottlenecks and implementing targeted automation solutions to address these challenges. As businesses expand, the agility provided by automation allows for rapid adaptation to changing market demands and operational requirements, ensuring sustainable growth.

Artificial Intelligence

The integration of AI and machine learning technologies has taken automation to new heights, particularly in enhancing customer experience and operational efficiency. AI-driven chatbots and virtual assistants can manage customer interactions 24/7, providing instant responses to inquiries, guiding users through the purchase process, and offering personalized recommendations, thereby elevating the customer service experience.

In operations, AI algorithms optimize logistics and supply chain management, predicting demand patterns, optimizing stock levels, and identifying the most efficient delivery routes. This not only reduces operational costs but also improves service delivery and customer satisfaction.

Furthermore, AI-powered analytics tools offer deep insights into customer behavior, market trends, and business performance. These insights enable data-driven decision-making, allowing businesses to refine their strategies and operations for better outcomes.

In conclusion, the power of automation lies in its ability to transform the way businesses operate, offering scalable solutions that drive efficiency, enhance customer experience, and foster growth. By embracing automation tools and AI technologies, businesses can navigate the complexities of the digital landscape more effectively, positioning themselves for success in an increasingly competitive market. The journey towards automation is a strategic investment in the future, unlocking new possibilities for innovation and sustainable business expansion.

Conclusion: Taking the Leap into Online Success

As we close the pages of "2023 Digital Gold Rush: Unleashing the Best Online Business Ideas and Niches From the Comfort of Your Home," it's clear that the digital landscape is ripe with opportunities for those willing to seize them. From the burgeoning fields of e-commerce and content creation to the dynamic realms of digital services, online education, affiliate marketing, remote consulting, and the transformative power of automation, the path to online success is diverse and accessible.

Recap of Key Opportunities and Strategies

- **E-commerce** has been demystified, highlighting various models like dropshipping, print-on-demand, and stocking inventory, each with its unique advantages and considerations.
- **Content Creation** emerged as a viable avenue for monetizing expertise and passions, with insights into leveraging platforms such as blogs, YouTube, and podcasts.
- **Digital Services**, including freelancing and consulting, were explored, showcasing

the demand for skills like digital marketing, web development, and graphic design.

- **Online Education** presented opportunities for sharing knowledge through courses, tapping into trends like microlearning and personalized content.
- **Affiliate Marketing** was revealed as a strategy for earning through partnerships, emphasizing the importance of choosing aligned products and optimizing for traffic and conversions.
- **Remote Consulting** underscored the potential in offering specialized knowledge across industries, from IT to health and wellness.
- **Automation** and AI were introduced as game-changers in streamlining operations and enhancing customer experiences, essential for scaling businesses efficiently.

Actionable Steps for Aspiring Entrepreneurs

- **Identify Your Niche**: Reflect on your skills, passions, and market demands to select a niche that resonates with you and has a clear audience.
- **Choose Your Model**: Decide on the business model that aligns with your goals, resources, and lifestyle. Whether it's

product-based, service-oriented, or content-driven, ensure it's something you can commit to and scale.

- **Build a Strong Foundation**: Invest time in creating a robust plan that includes market research, defining your target audience, and setting up the necessary tools and platforms.

- **Launch and Learn**: Start with a minimum viable product or service to gather feedback early on. Be prepared to iterate and improve based on customer input and market trends.

- **Embrace Marketing**: Develop a marketing strategy that leverages SEO, social media, email marketing, and content creation to build your brand and attract customers.

- **Automate and Scale**: Incorporate automation tools to streamline operations, allowing you to focus on growth activities. Consider expanding your product line, entering new markets, or hiring help as you scale.

Embrace the Digital Revolution

The journey into online entrepreneurship is both exhilarating and challenging. It requires courage, persistence, and a willingness to adapt. But the rewards—financial independence, flexibility, and the satisfaction of building something of your own—are immeasurable.

Remember, the digital world is constantly evolving, and so should you. Stay curious, continue learning, and remain open to new opportunities and technologies. Embrace the digital revolution with a proactive and positive mindset, and you'll find that the possibilities for success are as boundless as your ambition. Take the leap into online success, armed with the knowledge and strategies shared in this book. Your digital gold rush awaits—start your journey today and carve out your own path to triumph in the vibrant online economy.

Acknowledgments

I would like to express my deepest gratitude to the cherished individuals who have been instrumental in the creation of this book. Their unwavering support, encouragement, and love have been the guiding light throughout this journey.

First and foremost, I extend my heartfelt thanks to my dear mother, whose love, wisdom, and strength have been a constant source of inspiration. Her unwavering belief in me has fueled my passion for writing and has been a guiding force in every step of this endeavor.

To my beloved siblings, your love, support, and encouragement have been a cornerstone of my life. Your unwavering faith in my abilities has given me the confidence to pursue my dreams and turn them into reality. I am forever grateful for your presence in my life.

To my precious children, you are my greatest blessings and the driving force behind everything I do. Your boundless love, joy, and laughter have brought light into my darkest days, and I am endlessly grateful for the privilege of being your parent. May you always know how deeply loved and cherished you are.

Last but certainly not least, I extend my heartfelt appreciation to my dear spouse. Your unwavering support, patience, and understanding have been the bedrock of my success. Your belief in me has given me the courage to pursue my passions and dreams, and I am profoundly grateful for your constant presence by my side.

I would also like to thank my pastor for his exemplary leadership, guidance, and spiritual mentorship. Your wisdom, encouragement, and prayers have been a source of strength and inspiration, and I am deeply grateful for your unwavering dedication to serving the community and nurturing our faith.

To all those who have supported and encouraged me along this journey, whether through prayer, encouragement, or practical assistance, I offer my heartfelt thanks. Your kindness and generosity have touched my heart in ways words cannot express, and I am forever grateful for your presence in my life.

With deepest gratitude,

GO

About the Author

Grace is a remarkable woman whose life embodies a rich tapestry of roles and experiences. As a devoted follower of Christ, she radiates love, compassion, and faith in all aspects of her life. With a heart committed to serving others and a spirit grounded in the teachings of the Bible, she has touched countless lives with her kindness, wisdom, and grace.

As a mother, Grace finds her greatest joy and fulfillment in nurturing and guiding her children with love and wisdom. She approaches motherhood with unwavering dedication, seeking to instill in her children values of integrity, compassion, and faith that will guide them throughout their lives.

As a wife, Grace embodies the essence of partnership, love, and commitment. Her relationship with her spouse is characterized by mutual respect, understanding, and unwavering support. Together, they navigate life's challenges and joys with grace and unity, serving as a shining example of the beauty of marriage founded on faith and love.

As a daughter, Grace honors and cherishes the wisdom and guidance of her parents. She is deeply grateful for the values and principles instilled in her upbringing, which continue to shape her character and worldview. Her relationship with her parents is marked by love, respect, and gratitude for the sacrifices they have made to nurture and support her. As a sister, Grace treasures the bonds of family and friendship that have enriched her life. She shares a special connection with her siblings, built on a foundation of love, laughter, and shared experiences. Their relationship is a source of strength, support, and joy, reminding her of the power of familial love and unity.

As a friend, Grace embodies warmth, empathy, and compassion. She treasures the relationships she has formed with friends old and new, cherishing the moments of laughter, encouragement, and shared experiences. Her friendships are a testament to her ability to love and support others unconditionally, fostering deep connections built on trust and mutual respect.

As a businesswoman/entrepreneur, Grace brings a wealth of experience, skill, and determination to her endeavors. With a keen entrepreneurial spirit and a passion for excellence, she has achieved success in her professional pursuits, earning the respect and admiration of colleagues and clients alike. Her integrity, work ethic, and dedication to excellence set her apart as a leader in her field.

Finally, as a nurse, Grace embodies the spirit of compassion, care, and healing. Her career is a testament to her commitment to serving others and making a difference in the lives of those in need. With a heart for the sick and vulnerable, she approaches her work with empathy, professionalism, and unwavering dedication, earning the trust and gratitude of patients and colleagues alike.

In all aspects of her life, Grace shines as a beacon of faith, love, and compassion. Her journey is a testament to the transformative power of faith, the beauty of family and friendship, and the profound impact of serving others with love and humility. Through her words and actions, she continues to inspire and uplift those around her, leaving a lasting legacy of love, kindness, and grace.

www.ingramcontent.com/pod-product-compliance
Lightning Source LLC
Chambersburg PA
CBHW072327270726
48658CB00016B/2054